THE KEY
TO EPHESIANS

THE KEY
TO EPHESIANS

BY

Edgar J. Goodspeed

THE UNIVERSITY OF CHICAGO PRESS

Library of Congress Catalog Number: 56-6550

THE UNIVERSITY OF CHICAGO PRESS, CHICAGO 37
Cambridge University Press, London, N.W. 1, England
The University of Toronto Press, Toronto 5, Canada

© *1956 by The University of Chicago. Published 1956*
Second Impression 1957. Composed and printed by THE
UNIVERSITY OF CHICAGO PRESS, *Chicago, Illinois, U.S.A.*

INTRODUCTION

Some twenty years ago in our New Testament department at the University of Chicago I announced a seminar in the Letter to the Ephesians, and a small but really remarkable group of students responded. I had long tried to understand the letter as from the hand of Paul; but every time I taught it, the difficulties with that position, instead of disappearing or dwindling, grew in number and force until there was almost a score of them, and it began to dawn upon me that these were no longer to be regarded as difficulties; they were, in reality, clues to the solution of the leading problem in the Pauline literature. I have since listed them, in my ≪ Introduction to the New Testament,≫ of 1937, substantially as follows:

1. Ephesians reflects no definite, localized, historical situation which it is intended to meet.

2. The writer's admiration and regard for Paul are so emphasized in Ephesians that they give those who hold to the Pauline authorship some real difficulty (3:1-12). With all his great confidence in the importance of what he was doing, Paul did not himself evaluate his own activity in such sweeping and inclusive terms as these.

3. The writer's veneration for the holy apostles and prophets as the foundation of the church (2:20) and the mediums of revelation (3:5) is very different from Paul's view (I Cor. 3:11) that the church's one foundation is Christ himself. For Paul, Jesus Christ, the Messiah and Lord, is the only and the all-sufficient foundation for the church.

4. The church, in Ephesians, is always the church universal, not the individual, local church, but Paul uses the word in both senses (Gal. 1:13; I Cor. 16:19) and the local sense more frequently than the universal.

5. The church has become Greek, i.e., gentile, for the whole body of Christians addressed in 1:1 were once physically heathen (2:2, 11). There is no room for any Jewish Christianity in the picture. Christianity is now definitely a gentile religion.

6. The writer himself has been in the same condition (2:3) and is therefore a gentile Christian. In Romans, chaps. 1 and 2, Paul contrasts the sins

v

of Jews and Gentiles. It is the grosser, gentile sins that the writer now confesses for his readers and himself; compare II Cor. 11:22; Gal. 2:15; Phil. 3:4.

7. The encyclical form of the letter clearly implies a conception of Paul as a notable letter-writer, whose letters inherently deserve very wide circulation. This further implies that Paul's letters have already been collected as a corpus and are available for publication.

8. The sects are already beginning to appear (4:14), as in Acts 20:30, Rev. 2:6, 15. Hence the insistence on unity (4:3-6) as the prophylactic against divisiveness and sectarianism in the Christian group.

9. While much of the language is Pauline, it is used in other senses than Paul's. The "principalities and dominions" the Colossians were tempted to worship (1:16; 2:10) have in Ephesians become the spiritual enemies with which the Christian soldier must grapple (1:21; 6:12).

10. The style is reverberating and liturgical, not at all the direct, rapid Pauline give-and-take. Thus the Spirit, or the Holy Spirit, or the Spirit of God becomes "the holy Spirit of God" (4:30). Paul was a very effective popular preacher; he was not a liturgist.

11. The novel element in the vocabulary, that is, the words used in Ephesians, but not in the nine genuine letters of Paul, is mostly akin to the diction found in works like Luke-Acts, I Clement, I Peter, and Hebrews, written toward the close of the first century rather than in the vocabulary of earlier writings.

12. The interest in hymnology—the quotation of a Christian hymn, 5:14 —points to the time when that liturgical interest had begun to be active in the early church, as it is in the canticles of Luke (1:42, 46, 68; 2:14, 29) and in the arias, choruses, and antiphonies of the Revelation. This is a developing interest at the end of the first century.

13. The Descent into Hades (4:9, 10) is a difficult thing to fit into Paul's theology, since he virtually excludes it by what he says in Rom. 10:6, 7. It is akin to Luke's doctrine of the Ascension, delineated at the beginning of the second of his two volumes and reflected in Eph. 4:9.

14. This brings us to the use of the Acts in Ephesians, which thinks of Paul as where the Acts left him, a prisoner for the Greek mission, to which he had devoted his superlatively active career.

15. The reference to the breaking-down of the barrier that kept the heathen out of the Court of the Men of Israel in the Temple, while figurative, is more natural after the Temple had been destroyed in A.D. 70 than before that tragic denouement. Realistically, the wrecking of the Temple had eliminated that monumental barrier.

16. The jubilant review of the blessings of the Pauline salvation with which the letter begins is more natural in a reader of Paul's letters than in Paul himself. Paul's way was to take up one of them and dwell upon it. But in chapter 1 they fairly tumble over one another, with no full treatment of any of them. This is entirely natural if the collected letters of Paul, with full treatments of all of them, immediately followed.

17. The injunction of 6:4, to bring their children up with Christian training and instruction, is hardly like Paul; all he had to say on it in Col. 3:21 was, "Do not irritate your children." For Paul, expectations of the return of Jesus as the Messiah and of the establishment of God's kingdom are still too vivid and imminent to warrant the projection of long-term programs of religious education.

18. Ephesians is, on the whole, a generalization of Paulinism much more like a later Paulinist than like Paul himself. Someone has said it reads like a commentary on the letters of Paul. Even Romans, the most general of Paul's letters, is less of a generalization of Paul's positions than is Ephesians.

19. The writer of Ephesians is far more of an ecclesiastic than Paul was. He finds in the church a great spiritual fellowship, built upon the apostles and prophets, the medium of God's revelation, and the avenue of man's praise. It is the Bride of Christ, as in the Revelation, a little later, in the middle nineties.

20. Ephesians shows the unmistakable influence of every one of the nine genuine letters of Paul. These letters are all in existence. The writer of Ephesians knows them all, and knows them well. His familiarity with them, however, is not that of the apostolic author himself. It is rather the familiarity of a very admiring disciple of Paul.

21. Not only are all nine letters used in Ephesians, but, except for a few lines of Luke and Acts and some Septuagint texts, they fully supply all that it contains. Ephesians is almost completely a cento of the known letters of Paul.

Both Chrysostom and Calvin saw in Eph. 3:3 and 4 a reference to a subsequent reading of something that had been previously written. Obviously, they were right in this view of the matter. The testimony of the three great uncial manuscripts of Ephesians now clearly demonstrates this. These manuscripts specifically lack the words "in Ephesus" (vs. 1). Thus they render the document as a general communication, suitable for all Christians anywhere. Certainly the general letter to all would normally precede and introduce the letters written to the individual churches. This normal type of letter sequence is exemplified in the apocalyptic series of messages to the famous Seven Churches of Asia in Rev. 1-3. The bearing of that series on the problem of Ephesians and the Pauline letter collection has been generally neglected. There we have a precise reflection of the structure of the original Pauline letter corpus—a general letter to all the seven Pauline churches, followed by special messages to each of the seven.[1]

Previous investigators of Ephesians had pointed out a few parallels to its language, especially in Colossians and to a lesser extent in a few other major Pauline letters, but nothing systematic in this direction had been attempted. The high quality of the men in the Chicago seminar encouraged me to follow that clue further and to compare Ephesians in close detail with the nine generally accepted Pauline letters, Romans to Philemon, inquiring what other possible resemblances in thought or language might be observed. And to our surprise we found that not only Colossians but all the rest were substantially and unmistakably reflected and echoed in Ephesians! Even more than this, they supplied practically everything Ephesians contained, except a few scattered lines from the Acts or the Septuagint Old Testament. This bold position we took pains to support by a Greek table some eighty pages in length, showing the entire Greek text of Ephesians in one column, with the parallels in Colossians in the adjoining column, and two further columns showing the parallels in the other eight letters.

This exhibit, of course, proved the dependence of Ephesians on the nine Pauline letters; and, further, since Ephesians is one of the four letters of Paul clearly reflected in I Clement (A.D. 95), Ephesians would seem to have been a part of the Pauline letter collection from its first appearance. If one asks how these letters could affect a Gospel writer, let

---

1. On the extent to which ancient writers were stimulated to write books, by books previously written by others, see the « Journal of Biblical Literature, » LXIV (1945), 197-98.

John answer. He shows, forty years after Mark, what Paul's letters could do for one evangelist. Mark wrote probably at Rome, the scene of Paul's martyrdom. Matthew, ten years later, wrote probably from Antioch, Paul's first headquarters, and yet shows no acquaintance with any letters of his. This was the greatest literary period, 70-90, in early Christian history. In it the gospel type originated, the most effective form of religious instruction ever developed; and the early missionary movement was narrated in the comprehensive two-volume work of Luke. This book, with its matchless account of Paul and his labors may well have actually occasioned the (1) collecting, (2) completing, and (3) publishing of the Pauline letter collection as a whole.

For consider the facts. Mark, as we have seen, in his Gospel shows no acquaintance with a collection of Paul's letters. Matthew, about A.D. 80, writing probably at Antioch, shows no knowledge of such a collection. Some ten years later, Luke writes his Gospel, I suppose at Ephesus, still unacquainted with Paul's letters. Ephesus was the scene of Paul's longest ministry, and yet no Pauline letters! And then to crown these improbabilities, the Acts! Paul is the hero of the second part of Acts, and it contains pages of his addresses, none of them reflecting his letters or the characteristic ideas in them. How can this be explained? Of course, only by the fact that Paul's letters had not as yet been collected and published.

The fact is, the Corinthian Christians of the fifties would never have thought of publishing what we know as I Corinthians (Paul's very first letter to them they did not even preserve [I Cor. 5:9-13]). The idea that they would certainly publish it, of course loses sight of its sharply critical tone and the effect it is known to have produced at Corinth.—Or Galatians! Paul's "senseless Galatians"; he repeats it: "Are you so senseless?" The very critical tone of these two letters would have been keenly felt by their recipients, and it would have been strange indeed if they had been published in the lifetimes of their first recipients.

Of course, the wonder is that these letters, sometimes so sternly condemnatory that Paul himself afterward apologized (II Cor. 7:8-12), survived at all. Certainly they did not creep obscurely into publication, leaving no traces at Rome, Antioch, or Ephesus—the very places where, if they had been in circulation, they would have been sure to reach Mark, Matthew, or, above all, Luke. Yet he does not seem to know that Paul had ever written a letter; he evidently regarded any letters he might have written as minor matters. The failure of Luke to show any knowledge of them in his great picture of Paul in the Acts clearly shows that he was not acquainted with any Pauline letters at all. We cannot suppose that he preferred his own way of putting Christian truth and brushed Paul's aside. The earliest believers, moreover, were not contemplating a distant future; they were expecting the end of the world in a very short time and were in no literary mood at all. The idea of collecting and publishing Paul's letters would be totally out of place in such an atmosphere. Nor are his letters reflected at all anywhere before A.D. 90, when Ephesians shows the use of all nine of them.

It is a striking fact that while, up to about A.D. 90, no Christian writer had shown any acquaintance with Paul's writings, after that date every Christian writer did so! Nothing even in Acts, but after Acts—Ephesians, Revelation, I Clement, I Peter, Hebrews! All the further literature of the nineties shows the unmistakable influence of Paul's letters.

It is most unlikely that Ephesians had its own period of separate transmission as a single scroll, as some suggest. In 3:3 and 4, the reader is told to go on and read "what I have just briefly written." The logical meaning of this is that Ephesians is the Preface to Paul's collected letters; that is why it is so general, reflecting no particular church or situation and being addressed to Christians in general. The collection of ten letters, when first published, would form two Greek scrolls of ordinary length (just as Luke-Acts had so recently done) beginning with Ephesians, a general letter addressed to no particular church, as the oldest manuscripts conclusively show.

And what would Eph. 3:3, 4 mean, with nothing further for the reader to read? "As you read that, you will be able to understand the insight I have into the secret of the Christ." This sentence was so undervalued by the 1611 Revisers that, following the Geneva Bible of 1560 and the Bishops' of 1568, they reduced it to a parenthesis. RSV treats it as a reference to Ephesians itself. And yet RSV recognized Ephesians as a general letter, and such a letter could have been nothing but an introduction to the Pauline collection, as this sentence practically affirms. There can be no doubt that the corpus of letters to churches with which the Revelation soon after began reflects the organization of the Pauline corpus. (It even uses Paul's own distinctive form of salutation: "Blessing and peace to you"—without a verb!) In Revelation, the letters to the seven churches are prefaced by a general letter to all seven, which, in view of its use of Paul's peculiar form of salutation, can hardly have been anything but a following of the example of the recently published Pauline collection, with a general letter, known to us as Ephesians, as its introduction, and letters to seven churches following!

It is a natural suggestion that the martyrdom of Paul may have occasioned the collection and publication of his letters, somewhat as that of Peter, a very few years later, led to the writing of the Gospel of Mark; and, of course, that is the first possibility to explore. But with what result? No trace of the collected letters is to be found in the literature of the seventh, eighth, or ninth decades of the first century; the scrutiny of these decades yields nothing, though four of the longest and most important books in the New Testament were being written—Mark, Matthew, Luke, Acts. And it must not be forgotten that Galatians and the Corinthian letters gave very unfavorable pictures of those Christian groups, such as they themselves would hardly wish to have published. It is not until we reach the time immediately following the appearance of Luke-Acts that reflections of Paul's letters begin to appear in Christian writings, and we are driven to conclude that it was precisely then that the letters of Paul were collected and published. It must always be remembered that they were not meant for publication or for the public generally, being in great part personal and private or semiprivate in character, addressed to small church groups and discussing their problems, faults, and failings with the utmost frankness. Indeed, it is obvious that they could not be published in the lifetimes of the church members addressed; think of Galatians, or of I Cor. 1-6, or II Cor. 10-13! The wonder is that these letters were preserved at all, and, of course, a generation had to pass before they could decently be published. The men who insist that Paul's letters were so good that they must have been published right away show little realization of what they contain. That was just what could not be done.

Of Paul's letters, the Christian public of the eighties knew nothing. How should they have known them? They were intimate letters, to somebody else. Their collection was anything but a matter of course; it was a most unusual and providential undertaking, so rare in the ancient world as to be almost unparalleled. Pliny's careful preservation, for subsequent polishing and publication, of his own best letters is no parallel; Paul did not preserve, correct, polish, and later publish his letters! That Paul's semiprivate letters to half-a-dozen churches should, thirty years after his death, have been unearthed and published is an extraordinary thing in Christian history and by no manner of means the ordinary, inevitable, commonplace matter-of-course it is sometimes taken to be.

What must be explained is the total eclipse of Paul's letters until after the appearance of the Acts, when they burst upon the churches in all their vigor, and shaped or colored their literature ever after. It is, moreover, very striking that much as the Acts makes of Paul—Luke's hero, the supreme Christian missionary—it never mentions one of his letters and seems never to have heard of his writing one! We must carefully distinguish the two different things: Paul the tireless, indomitable Christian missionary and Paul the writer of corrective letters to faraway churches. The former, the churches did not forget; the latter, most of them had never even heard of. Paul did not go about advertising the fact that he had written a long, long letter to the Corinthians or the Romans. He had more pressing things to say to the people who heard him.

The extent to which the writer of Ephesians reproduces Colossians is most naturally explained if he had long been acquainted with it, as he might well have been if he had grown up in the Colossae-Laodicea-Hierapolis circle—the towns were in sight of one another and almost formed one community. Such a man, long steeped in familiarity with Colossians and Philemon, as we call the letter to the neighboring church of Laodicea, but unaware of any other letters written by Paul, might well be led by the narrative of Acts to the startling idea that there might possibly be other letters of Paul still in existence in the church chests of Rome, Galatia, Corinth, Thessalonica, or Philippi, as he knew there were at Colossae. And when, acting upon this suggestion, he had recovered seven of them and came to write his introductory general letter, of course his memory was full of the letter he had known so long and knew perhaps almost by heart—Colossians.

It is most gratifying to find this solution of the Ephesians problem cordially adopted in England and reproduced, table and all, with further extensions at Oxford. Recent American discussion brings out the fact that often in the writer's use of the other Pauline letters he has blended and conflated phrases from two of them to make his own expression. This is a striking confirmation of our theory of Ephesians' origin.

The book of Acts itself seems to have made some contribution to the vocabulary of Ephesians. The word "halusis," "chain," is not found in the nine Pauline letters but occurs four times in the Acts, in three of these being used of Paul; it is used once in Ephesians. Paul himself used "desmos" seven times. It is also a frequent word in the Acts. "Evangelist" is found once in Acts, once in Ephesians; never in Paul, but later in the Pastorals. "Diabolos" never occurs in Paul; it is found twice in the Acts and once in Ephesians; Paul uses "Satan" eight times. "Panoplia" occurs once in Luke, twice in Eph. 6; nowhere else in the New Testament.

These are small details, but the commanding fact is that it is the hero of Acts 13-28 whose nine letters are collected and published immediately after the appearance of Luke-Acts. This reinforces the lexical evidence of these few words. For we can hardly suppose that the appearance of Luke-Acts had no relation to the collecting of the letters of Paul.

Picture the situation: An Asian Christian, long possessed of Colossians and Philemon (for Paul had expressly written the Colossians to read the letter from Laodicea [Col. 4:16]), would see in the narrative of Acts the possibility of further letters. Acts could, and obviously did, tell him where to look for possible further church letters of Paul, to find Galatians, Philippians, Thessalonians, Corinthians, and Romans. It is worth noting that Paul had himself involuntarily given an initial impulse for the collecting of his letters when he told the Colossians (4:16) to share that letter with the Laodiceans, and to "read the letter that is coming from there." The nucleus of the Pauline collection already lay in the church chests of those churches, in Colossians and Laodiceans (Philemon).

A hasty glance at our tables of parallels may suggest that some at least of the parallels indicated have no great evidential value. This is quite true. For when we had found enough to convince us of the literary dependence of Ephesians upon the nine genuine Pauline letters, we went on to record any other parallels that might appear, as therefore presumably from the same source. This led us to the surprising conclusion with which I began these remarks. For it seemed to us that if Ephesians demonstrably draws its leading, characteristic, and most powerful elements from the nine Pauline letters, then any further material, however slight, which they may parallel may well have come from them and thus been made to add to the genuinely Pauline atmosphere of the new letter.

Such a letter was needed to introduce these letters of a former generation to Christians of the year A.D. 90. Much had happened since Paul's ministry and death. The situations that faced the churches in the nineties were not those of the fifties. The expectation of Jesus' immediate return in apocalyptic judgment, though so soon reinforced by the Revelation of John, did not possess its old original power. The problems of the Thessalonians, the Corinthians, and the Galatians, which had been so peculiarly theirs, were, after forty years, getting out of date. And yet there were tremendous values in these old letters, and Paul's powerful enforcement of the Christian's duties and privileges had not grown old. To call attention to these great values and point the believers of the tenth decade to Paul's masterly exposition of them called for a strong introduction, which should set forth Paul's great characteristic presentations of the supreme values of the Christian faith. That is what Ephesians so nobly undertook, and achieved, and in the name of Paul, since every sentence of it owed its vital quality to him. So the great values of the Christian faith, stripped of their local and immediate applications in the letters of Paul, emerge in a form more suitable to the new age, with its new demands and new exigencies.

We have not failed to validate this approach to Ephesians by applying the same test to another letter, accepted as of Pauline authorship. Lest we be misled by our own ingenuity, we compared the second chapter of Philippians in close detail with the other accepted letters of Paul, to see if it, too, was as fully indebted to them as we have shown Ephesians to be. More recently, in England, such a survey was extended by C. Leslie Mitton to all of Philippians, and with the same result, shown in his "Epistle to the Ephesians: Its Authorship, Origin, and Purpose" (Oxford, 1951). Philippians shows no such degree of dependence on the other letters of Paul as Ephesians does. The contrast is pronounced. We approached this very stiff task with no presumption as to its outcome, but with minds open to the evidence that should emerge. It is gratifying to find that British learning has accepted our method and pursued it with even greater fulness and with results substantially the same as our own.

It is, of course, tempting to pursue the process in relation to names and persons as well. It is a well-known fact that the bishop of Ephesus in Ignatius' day (A.D. 110-17) was named Onesimus (≪ Ignatius to the Ephesians, ≫ 1:3; 2:1; 6:2) and that he and Polycarp, bishop of Smyrna, aided and stimulated Ignatius to write his seven letters, six of them to churches on or near his route, and one to Polycarp. Fifty years before, Paul had a young protégé named Onesimus, who came from Laodicea and was himself the subject of the Letter to Philemon. Paul saw in him considerable possibilities, and it is certainly true that no one is more likely to have cherished that letter and Colossians, which accompanied it, than that young man. When we recognize in them, especially in Colossians, the nucleus of the Pauline letter collection, we cannot help wondering whether it was not that same Onesimus, who had so long cherished a letter or two of his great benefactor, who was aroused by Luke's great book which made so much of Paul, to begin the search for Paul's letters in his other fields of labor and thus to become the maker of the collection and perhaps even the writer of the introduction. I don't know how this mere conjecture may strike the reader, but it fills my eyes with tears. The emancipated slave lives to build his protector a monument more enduring than bronze! Why, whoever he was, he made Paul a lasting force in Christianity, second only to Jesus himself!

More than one New Testament scholar has observed that he felt a deep inward conviction that the writer of Ephesians must have been a personal follower of Paul, and that may well be true.

Furthermore, would it not be like a man who had accomplished the collection of Paul's scattered letters of other years to stimulate Ignatius, bishop of Antioch, a "confessor" on his way to Rome for martyrdom, to write letters to the churches on or near his route—and then to collect these letters—of course for publication? That was what Onesimus, bishop of Ephesus, did some twenty years later with the aid of Polycarp, bishop of Smyrna, a city hardly fifty miles from Ephesus, as the crow flies. What can be more likely than that the man who stimulated the writing, collecting, and circulating of the seven letters of Ignatius was the very man who had already led in collecting and publishing the Pauline letters, twenty years before? Those letters were sweeping the Christian world in Ignatius' day. I see no improbability in the idea that the youth who had so interested Paul at Rome that he exerted himself to have him emancipated should have cherished the letters which had freed him and even organized the search for further letters of Paul and the publication of them, providing them all with an admirable introduction, and later, becoming bishop of Ephesus, should have stimulated Ignatius to write letters to the churches on his route to Rome and seen to their publication also.

Is it any easier historically to suppose four different men did these four similar things, evidently in the same place (Ephesus), especially when the fourth has the same name as the first, and for the other two no names are recorded? Ephesus was, as Harnack used to say, the second fulcrum of Christianity. The correspondence of Ignatius discloses to us Onesimus, bishop of Ephesus, as an important functionary at that fulcrum.

A singular corroboration of this extraordinary story is the fact that Ignatius in his Letter to the Ephesians, chapters 1-6, is full of clear allusions to the Letter to Philemon, as John Knox has shown in his ≪ Philemon among the Letters of Paul ≫ (Chicago, 1935). Indeed, the neglect and careless treatment that scholars have shown Philemon becomes more and more regrettable when it is realized what a key they had in their hands. Lake in his "Introduction" gives Philemon nine lines, and Vincent in his commentary (p. 192) mistakes the people sending salutations for those to whom they were sent, thus completely confusing the problem of where they were and where the writer was.

This tempting identification of the writer of Ephesians, probable as it is, is still conjecture. What is certain is that Ephesians is based upon the nine genuine letters of Paul and fashioned out of them, by a skilful and gifted hand, to serve as an introduction for them to the churches of the next generation. The great Vatican and Sinaitic manuscripts of the early fourth century do not have the phrase "in Ephesus" from the first hand; it was written in, long after, between the lines! And since this table of resemblances was first published, in Greek, in 1933, the same reading, that is, the omission of "in Ephesus," has been found in the Michigan papyrus of the letters of Paul, from the first years of the third century. Such decisive negative evidence is an extraordinary confirmation of the great fourth-century uncials and of the encyclical character of the Letter to the Ephesians, for which this study offers an explanation.

To make the literary relationships of Ephesians plain to a wider public, the exhibit of its resemblances to Paul's own nine letters is here presented in English—the English of the American Standard Version of 1901. This version is, in general, so scrupulous about translating every occurrence of a Greek word by the same English word, if at all possible, that, for purposes of close comparison, it is almost as good as the Greek itself.

EPHESIANS	COLOSSIAN PARALLELS
1	1:1, 2

1 Paul,
   an apostle of Christ Jesus
   through the will of God,
   to the saints
   that are at Ephesus,
   and the faithful
   in Christ Jesus:

Paul,
   an apostle of Christ Jesus
   through the will of God, . . .
   to the saints

   and faithful brethren
   in Christ
   that are at Colossae:

2 Grace to you and peace
   from God our Father
   and the Lord Jesus Christ.

Grace to you and peace
   from God our Father.

3 Blessed be the God and Father
   of our Lord Jesus Christ,
   who hath blessed us

with every spiritual blessing

in the heavenly places in Christ:

                                         3:12b

4 even as he chose us in him   as God's elect,

before the foundation of the world,[1]

                                           1:22b

that we should be holy   to present you holy

and without blemish before him in love: and without blemish . . . before him:

5 having foreordained us

unto adoption as sons

through Jesus Christ

unto himself,

---

1. Lk. 11:50.

OTHER PAULINE PARALLELS

II Cor. 1:1-3

Paul,
an apostle of Christ Jesus
through the will of God, . . .
with all the saints
that are in the whole of Achaia:

Grace to you and peace
from God our Father
and the Lord Jesus Christ.
Blessed be the God and Father
of our Lord Jesus Christ,
the Father of mercies

Gal. 3:14a
that upon the Gentiles might come the
blessing of Abraham in Christ Jesus:

Rom. 1:11b
that I may impart unto you some spiritual gift,

and God of all comfort;

Cf. Phil. 2:10; I Cor. 15:40-49

I Cor. 1:27a
but God chose the foolish things of the
world,

I Cor. 2:7b
which God foreordained before the
worlds unto our glory:

II Thess. 2:13b
for that God chose you

from the beginning unto salvation

in sanctification of the Spirit and be-
lief of the truth:

Cf. Rom. 5:1-11

Rom. 8:29
For whom he foreknew,
he also foreordained to be

Gal. 4:5b
that we might re-
ceive
the adoption of
sons.

Gal. 3:26
For ye are all

conformed to the image

of his Son, that he might be the firstborn
among many brethren:

Cf. Rom. 8:15, 25

sons of God,
through faith, in
Christ Jesus.

EPHESIANS	COLOSSIAN PARALLELS
1	
according to the good pleasure of his will,	
6 to the praise of the glory of his grace,	
which he freely bestowed on us	
	1:13b, 14a
in the Beloved:	the Son of his love;
7 in whom we have our redemption	in whom we have our redemption,
	1:20b
	having made peace
through his blood,	through the blood of his cross;
	1:14b
the forgiveness of our trespasses,	the forgiveness of our sins:
according to the riches	
of his grace,	
	1:9b
8 which he made to abound	that ye may be filled with the knowledge of his will
toward us in all wisdom and prudence,	in all spiritual wisdom and understanding,
	1:27a
9 making known unto us	to whom God was pleased to make known what is the riches of the glory
the mystery of his will,	of this mystery among the Gentiles,
according to his good pleasure	
which he purposed in him	
	1:25b; cf. 26
10 unto a dispensation	according to the dispensation of God

OTHER PAULINE PARALLELS

Phil. 2:13

for it is God who worketh in you both to will
and to work, for his good pleasure.

Phil. 1:11b

which are through Jesus Christ,
unto the glory and praise
of God

Rom. 5:15b

much more did the grace of God, and the gift
by the grace
of the one man, Jesus Christ, abound unto
the many.

Rom. 5:9b

being now justified

by his blood,

II Cor. 5:19b

not reckoning unto them their trespasses,

Rom. 2:4a

Or despisest thou the riches

of his goodness

Rom. 11:33a

O the depth of the riches

both of the wisdom and the knowledge of
God!

I Cor. 2:7a

but we speak God's wisdom

in a mystery,

Rom. 8:28b

Cf. Phil. 2:13b above

called according to his purpose.

I Cor. 2:7b

which God foreordained

Cf. Rom. 5:1-11

II Cor. 9:14b, 15

by reason of the exceeding
grace of God

in you. Thanks be to God

for his unspeakable gift.

Rom. 3:25, 26a

whom God set forth to be a propitiation,

through faith, in his blood,
to show his righteousness because
of the passing over of the sins done
aforetime,
in the forebearance of God;

Rom. 5:15b

much more did the grace of God, and
the gift by the grace of the one man,
Jesus Christ, abound

unto the many.

Rom. 16:25b, 26a

according to the revelation (see below)

of the mystery which hath been kept in
silence . . .
but now . . .
according to the commandment of the
eternal God, is made known

EPHESIANS	COLOSSIAN PARALLELS
1	
of the fulness of the times,	to fulfil the word of God,
	1:20; cf. 1:18; 2:10
	and through him
to sum up all things in Christ,	to reconcile all things unto himself, . . .
	through him, I say,
the things in the heavens,	whether things upon the earth,
and the things upon the earth;	or things in the heavens.
11 in him, I say, in whom also	
	1:12b
we were made a heritage,	who made us meet to be partakers of the inheritance of the saints in light;
having been foreordained	
according to the purpose of him	
who worketh all things	
after the counsel of his will;	
12 to the end that we should be unto the praise of his glory,	
we who had before hoped in Christ:	
	1:5b, 6a
13 in whom ye also, having heard	whereof ye heard before
the word of the truth,	in the word of the truth
the gospel of your salvation,—	of the gospel, which is come unto you;
in whom, having also believed,	

OTHER PAULINE PARALLELS

Gal. 4:4a

when the fulness of the time came,

Rom. 13:9b

it is summed up in this word,   Cf. I Cor. 15:27

Rom. 8:30a

and whom he foreordained, . . .

Rom. 8:28b

to them that are called   Rom. 9:11b

according to his purpose.   that the purpose of God . . . might stand.

I Cor. 12:6b   Phil. 2:13

who worketh all things in all.   it is God who worketh in you

Rom. 9:19b

For who withstandeth his will?   both to will and to work, for his good

pleasure.

Gal. 1:4b

according to the will of our God and

Father:

Rom. 9:23, 24   Phil. 1:11b

that he might make known   unto the glory and praise of God.

the riches of his glory upon vessels of   Rom. 8:30c

mercy,   them he also glorified.

which he afore prepared unto glory, even

us, whom he also called, not from the

Jews only,   Rom. 10:14b

but also from the Gentiles?   and how shall they believe

II Cor. 6:7a

in the word of truth,

Rom. 1:16b

the gospel: for it is the power of God

unto salvation

to every one that believeth;   in him whom they have not heard?

EPHESIANS	COLOSSIAN PARALLELS
1	
ye were sealed	
with the Holy Spirit of promise,	
14 which is an earnest	1:12b
	Who made us meet to be
of our inheritance,	partakers of the inheritance of the saints
	in light;
	1:14a
unto the redemption	in whom we have our redemption,
of God's own possession,	
unto the praise of his glory.	
	1:9a
15 For this cause I also,	For this cause we also, since the day we
	heard it,
	1:4
having heard of the faith	having heard of your faith
in the Lord Jesus	in Christ Jesus,
which is among you,	
and the love which ye show	and of the love which ye have
toward all the saints,	toward all the saints,
	1:9
16 cease not to give thanks for you,	we . . . do not cease to pray
making mention of you	and make request for you,
	1:3
in my prayers;	We give thanks
17 that the God	to God the Father
of our Lord Jesus Christ,	of our Lord Jesus Christ,
	praying always for you,
the Father of glory,	
may give unto you	that ye may be filled

OTHER PAULINE PARALLELS

I Cor. 1:22; cf. 5:5
who also sealed us,
and gave us the earnest

of the Spirit in our hearts.

Gal. 3:14b
that we might receive
the promise of the Spirit through faith.
Rom. 8:16, 17a
The Spirit himself beareth witness
with our spirit, that we are children
of God: and if children, then heirs;

Rom. 8:23b
waiting for our adoption, . . .
the redemption of our body.

I Thess. 5:9b
unto the obtaining of salvation
Phil. 1:11b
unto the glory and praise of God.

Rom. 1:8
First, I thank my God through Jesus Christ
for you all,

that your faith is proclaimed
throughout the whole world.

Philem. 5
hearing of thy love,
and of the faith which thou

hast toward the Lord Jesus,

and toward all the saints;

Phil. 1:3, 4a
I thank my God upon all

my remembrance of you,

Philem. 4	Rom. 1:9b, 10a
I thank my God al-ways,	how unceasingly
making mention of thee	I make mention of you,
	always in my prayers
in my prayers	making request,

always in every supplication of mine on
behalf of you all
II Cor. 11:31a
The God and Father
of the Lord Jesus,
Rom. 6:4b
through the glory of the Father,

II Cor. 1:3b	I Cor. 2:8b
the Father of mer-cies	the Lord of glory

I Cor. 2:10a
But unto us God

EPHESIANS	COLOSSIAN PARALLELS
1	with the knowledge of his will
a spirit of wisdom and revelation	in all spiritual wisdom and understanding,
in the knowledge of him;	
18 having the eyes of your heart	
	1:12b
enlightened,	to be partakers of the inheritance of the saints in light;
	1:26b, 27
that ye may know what is the hope of his calling, what the riches of the glory of his inheritance in the saints,	but now hath it been manifested to his saints, to whom God was pleased to make known what is the riches of the glory of this mystery among the Gentiles, which is Christ in you, the hope of glory:
19 and what the exceeding greatness	
	1:11a
of his power	strengthened with all power,
to us-ward who believe,	
according to that working of the strength of his might	according to the might of his glory,
	1:29b
	according to his working,
20 which he wrought in Christ,	which worketh in me mightily.
	Cf. 2:12
when he raised him from the dead,	
	3:1b
	the things that are above,
and made him to sit	where Christ is, seated
at his right hand[2] in the heavenly places,	on the right hand of God.
	2:10b
21 far above all rule, and authority,	who is the head of all

---

2. Ps. 110:1.

OTHER PAULINE PARALLELS

Rom. 16:25b

according to

the revelation of the mystery

Rom. 1:28b

to have

God in their knowledge,

revealed them

through the Spirit:

Rom. 1:21b

and their senseless heart was darkened.

II Cor. 4:4b

that the light of the gospel . . . should not

dawn

Rom. 9:23a

that he might make known

the riches of his glory

II Cor. 9:14b

the exceeding grace of God in you

Phil. 3:10b

the power of his resurrection

Rom. 3:22b

unto all them that believe;

Phil. 3:21b

according to the working whereby he is able

even to subject all things unto himself.

Rom. 8:34

It is Christ Jesus that

died, yea rather, that

was raised from the dead,

I Cor. 6:14

and God both raised the Lord,

and will raise up us

through his power.

Phil. 2:9, 10

Wherefore also God highly exalted him, and

gave unto him the name

who is

at the right hand of God,

Cf. I Cor. 15:40-49

I Cor. 15:24b

which is above

when he shall have abolished all rule,

EPHESIANS	COLOSSIAN PARALLELS
1	
and power, and dominion,	principality and power:
	1:16b
	whether thrones or dominions or principalities or powers;
and every name that is named,	
not only in this world, but also in that which is to come:	
22 and he put all things in subjection under his feet,[3]	
	1:18a
and gave him to be head over all things	And he is the head of the body,
to the church,	the church:
23 which is his body,	1:19
	For it was the good pleasure of the Father that in him
the fulness	should all the fulness dwell;
of him that filleth all in all.[4]	Cf. 1:16, 17

---

3. Ps. 8:6.
4. Jer. 23:24b.

OTHER PAULINE PARALLELS

and all authority and power.

every name; that in the name of Jesus
every knee should bow, of things in heaven

                                 I Cor. 2:6b
                      yet a wisdom
and things on earth   not of this world,
and things under the earth,   Cf. Rom. 8:38b
                                   I Cor. 12:27b
          Cf. vs. 10 above   For, He put all things
                      in subjection under his feet.

          Rom. 12:5a
so we, who are many,   I Cor. 12:27a
are one body in Christ,   Now ye are the body of Christ,

          Rom. 11:36a   I Cor. 15:28b
For of him, and through him,   that God may be
and unto him, are all things.   all in all.

EPHESIANS 2	COLOSSIAN PARALLELS
1 And you <u>did he make alive</u>,	2:13a
when ye were dead	And you,
through your trespasses and sins,	being dead
	through your trespasses
	3:7a
2 wherein ye once walked	wherein ye also once walked,
according to the course	
of this world,	
according to the prince	
of the powers of the air,	1:13a
	out of the power of darkness,
of the spirit that now worketh	
	3:6b
in the sons of disobedience;	upon the sons of disobedience:
	3:7
3 among whom we also all	wherein ye also
once lived	once walked, when ye lived
	in these things;
	1:21
in the lusts of our flesh,	And you, being in time past alienated
doing the desires of the flesh	and enemies
and of the mind,	in your mind
	in your evil works,
and were by nature	
	3:6b
children of wrath,	cometh the wrath of God upon
	the sons of disobedience:
even as the rest:—	

OTHER PAULINE PARALLELS

Rom. 6:11b
reckon ye also yourselves
to be dead
unto sin,

Rom. 12:2a
according to this world:

I Cor. 2:12b
But we received,
not the spirit of the world,

Cf. II Thess. 2:3b, 4a
the man of sin . . .
the son of perdition,
he that opposeth

Cf. I Cor. 2:6, 8

II Thess. 2:7a
For the mystery of lawlessness
doth already work:

I Thess. 2:13b
which also worketh

Rom. 15:31a; cf. 11:30
from them that are disobedient

in you that believe.

Rom. 3:23; cf. 3:9
for all have sinned, and
fall short of the glory of God;

II Cor. 1:12b
we behaved ourselves in the world,

Rom. 1:24b
in the lusts of their hearts

Rom. 15:14b; cf. Gal. 5:16, 24
and make not provision for the flesh, to
fulfil the lusts thereof.

Rom. 8:7; cf. Gal. 5:19
the mind of the flesh is enmity
against God:

Cf. Gal. 2:15a
We being Jews by nature,

Gal. 4:28b
Now we . . . are

I Thess. 5:9a
For God
appointed us not unto wrath,

I Thess. 4:13b
even as the rest,
who have no hope.

children of promise.

EPHESIANS	COLOSSIAN PARALLELS
2	
4 but God, being rich in mercy,	
for his great love	
wherewith he loved us,	
	2:13a
5 even when we were dead	And you, being dead
through our trespasses,	through your trespasses . . .
made us alive together with	did he make alive together with
Christ	him,
(by grace have ye been saved),	
	2:12b
	wherein
	ye were also raised with him
6 and raised us up with him,	3:1a
	If then ye were raised together with Christ,
	3:3
	For ye died, and your life is hid with
and made us to sit with him	Christ in God.
	3:1b
in the heavenly <u>places</u>,	seek the things that are above,
in Christ Jesus:	where Christ is,
	seated on the right hand of God.
7 that in the ages to come	
he might show	
the exceeding riches	
of his grace	
in kindness toward us	
	1:4b
in Christ Jesus:	in Christ Jesus,
8 for by grace	
have ye been saved	

OTHER PAULINE PARALLELS

Rom. 11:32b, 33a
that he might have mercy upon all. O
the depth of the riches . . . of God!

Rom. 5:8; cf. 5:5; 8:39
God commendeth his own love toward us,
in that, while we were yet sinners,
Christ died for us.

II Thess. 2:16b
God our Father who loved us

Cf. Rom. 8:10

Rom. 3:24a
being justified freely by his grace

Cf. Rom. 6:5, 8, 11

Cf. Phil. 5:20; 2:10	Cf. I Cor. 15:40
Rom. 9:23a	
and that	
he might make known	Rom. 2:4a (Cf. II Cor. 9:14)
	Or despisest thou
the riches	the riches
of his glory	
upon vessels of mercy,	of his goodness
Rom. 3:24; cf. chaps. 3-5	Rom. 8:24a
being justified freely	For in hope
by his grace	were we saved:

EPHESIANS 2	COLOSSIAN PARALLELS
through faith;	
and that not of yourselves,	
it is the gift of God;	
9 not of works,	
that no man should glory.	
10 For we are his workmanship,	
created in Christ Jesus	Cf. 3:9, 10
	1:10a
	to walk worthily of the Lord . . .
	bearing fruit in every good work,
	Cf. 1:21b
for good works,	in your evil works,
which God afore prepared	
that we should walk in them.	Cf. 1:10a above
	4:18b
11 Wherefore remember, that	Remember my bonds.
	Cf. 2:11
once ye, the Gentiles in the flesh,	in whom ye
who are called Uncircumcision by that which is called	
Circumcision, in the flesh,	were also circumcised with a circumcision
made by hands;	not made with hands, in the putting off of the body of the flesh, in the circumcision of Christ;

OTHER PAULINE PARALLELS

Rom. 3:28
We reckon therefore that
a man is justified by faith

through the redemption
that is in Christ Jesus:

Rom. 6:23b; cf. 5:15b; 3:24
but the free gift of God is eternal   (Cf. Rom. 5:15b; 6:23b)
life in Christ Jesus our Lord.
Rom. 9:32b
not by faith, but as it were by works.   apart from the works of the law.
I Cor. 1:29, 30a
that no flesh should glory before God.   Cf. Rom. 3:27
But of him are ye

                           II Cor. 5:17a
in Christ Jesus,   if any man is in Christ, he is
Rom. 13:3a   a new creature: Cf. Gal. 6:15 below
rulers are not a terror

                           II Cor. 9:8b
to the good work,   unto every good work:

Cf. Rom. 8:29a
For whom he foreknew,
he also foreordained
I Cor. 12:2a
Ye know that

when ye were Gentiles   Cf. Rom. 11:17
Cf. I Cor. 8:5a
there be that are called gods,

Gal. 6:15   Rom. 2:28b; cf. vss. 26-29
For neither is circumcision   neither is that circumcision
anything, nor uncircumcision,   which is outward in the flesh:
but a new creature.   Cf. Phil. 3:3

EPHESIANS	COLOSSIAN PARALLELS
2	**1:21a**
12 that ye were at that time	And you, being in time past
separate from Christ,	
alienated from	alienated and enemies
	in your mind in your evil works,
the commonwealth of Israel,	
and strangers from	
the covenants of the promise,	
having no hope	
and without God	
in the world.	
	1:22a; cf. 3:11
13 But now	yet now hath he reconciled
in Christ Jesus	
ye that once were far off	
are made nigh	
in the blood of Christ.	in the body of his flesh
	through death
	1:20b
14 For he is our peace,[1]	having made peace through
	the blood of his cross;
who made both one,	
and brake down	
the middle wall of partition,	
	2:14a
15 having abolished	having blotted out
	1:21b
in his flesh the enmity,	enemies in your mind

---

1. Isa. 57:19b

Peace, peace, to him that is far off
and to him that is near.

OTHER PAULINE PARALLELS

Cf. Rom. 1:28-32

Gal. 5:4a
Ye are severed from Christ,

Rom. 9:4
who are Israelites; whose is the adoption,
and. . . .
the covenants, . . . and the promises;
    I Thess. 4:13b
even as the rest,
who have no hope.
    I Thess. 4:5b
even as the Gentiles
who know not God;

Gal. 4:8, 9a
Howbeit at that time,
not knowing God,
ye were in bondage to them
that by nature are no gods:

    Cf. I Cor. 4:9b
for we are made a spectacle
unto the world,
    Gal. 3:28b; cf. 28a
for ye all are one <u>man</u>

but now that ye have come
to know God,

in Christ Jesus.

    Rom. 5:1b
we have peace with God
through our Lord Jesus Christ;
    Gal. 3:28c
for ye are all one <u>man</u>
in Christ Jesus.
    Gal. 3:28a
There can be neither
Jew nor Greek,

EPHESIANS	COLOSSIAN PARALLELS
2	2:14a
	having blotted out
even the law of commandments	the bond
contained in ordinances;	written in ordinances
	that was against us,
that he might create in himself	
	3:9b, 10a
of the two	ye have put off the old man with
	his doings, and have put on
one new man,	the new man,
	1:19b, 20a
	and through him to reconcile
	all things
	unto himself,
so making peace;	having made peace
	through the blood of his cross,
	1:22
16 and might reconcile them both	yet now hath he reconciled
in one body	in the body of his flesh
unto God	
through the cross,	through death,
	to present you . . .
	before him:
having slain the enmity thereby:	
17 and he came and preached	
peace to you that were far off,	
and peace to them that were nigh:[2]	
18 for through him	
we both have our access	
in one Spirit unto the Father.	

---

2. Isa. 57:19 (cf. 52:7b):
Peace, peace to him that is far off
and to him that is near.

OTHER PAULINE PARALLELS

Gal. 3:28 above

for ye are all

one <u>man</u> in Christ Jesus.

I Cor. 12:13a
For in one Spirit were we
all baptized into one body,

Rom. 5:2a
through whom also
we have had our access by faith

into this grace wherein we stand;

I Cor. 12:13a
For in one Spirit were we all baptized into one body,
Phil. 1:27b
that ye stand fast in one spirit,

EPHESIANS	COLOSSIAN PARALLELS
2	3:11a
19 So then ye are no more	where there cannot be
	Greek and Jew, circumcision
strangers and sojourners,	and uncircumcision, barbarian,
	Scythian, bondman, freeman;
but ye are fellow-citizens	
with the saints,	
and of the household of God,	
20 being	
	2:7b
built upon the foundation	builded up
of the apostles and prophets,[3]	
Christ Jesus himself	in him,
	2:19b
being the chief corner stone;	the Head,
21 in whom	from whom
each several building,	all the body,
fitly framed together,	being supplied and knit together
	through the joints and bands,
groweth	increaseth
into a holy temple	
in the Lord;	with the increase of God.
22 in whom ye also	
	2:7b
are builded together	builded up in him,
for a habitation of God	
in the Spirit.	

---

3. Acts 13: 1b; 15:6b.

OTHER PAULINE PARALLELS

Phil. 3:20a
For our citizenship is in heaven;

Gal. 6:10b
of the household of the faith.

I Cor. 12:28a
And God

I Cor. 3:11a
For other foundation can no man lay

hath set some in the church,
first apostles, secondly prophets,
I Cor. 3:10, 11b
I laid a foundation;
and another buildeth thereon.

than that which is laid,
which is Jesus Christ.

I Cor. 3:9b
ye are . . . God's building.

I Cor. 3:6b
but God gave the increase.
I Cor. 3:16b
ye are a temple of God,
I Cor. 3:7b
but God that giveth the increase.

II Cor. 6:16b
for we are a temple

of the living God;

I Cor. 3:16b
the Spirit of God dwelleth in you

Rom. 8:9
But ye are not in the flesh
but in the Spirit,
if so be that the Spirit of God
dwelleth in you.

EPHESIANS	COLOSSIAN PARALLELS
3	
1 For this cause I Paul,	
the prisoner of Christ Jesus	
	1:24a
	Now I rejoice in my sufferings
in behalf of you Gentiles,—	for your sake,
2 if so be that ye have heard	
	1:25b
of the dispensation	according to the dispensation
of that grace of God	of God
which was given me	which was given me
to you-ward;	to you-ward,
3 how that by revelation	
was made known unto me	
	1:26a
the mystery	even the mystery
as I wrote before in few words,	4:16a
4 whereby, when ye read,	And when this epistle hath been read among you
	1:9b
ye can perceive my understanding	that ye may be filled with the knowledge of his will in all spiritual wisdom and understanding,
	4:3b
in the mystery of Christ;	the mystery of Christ,
	1:26b
5 which in other generations	which hath been hid
was not made known	for ages and generations:

OTHER PAULINE PARALLELS

II Cor. 10:1

I Paul

Philem. 1

Paul,
a prisoner of Christ Jesus,

Rom. 11:13a

But I speak
to you that are Gentiles.

Gal. 1:13a

For ye have heard of my manner of life
in time past

I Cor. 9:17b

but if not of mine own will,
I have a stewardship intrusted to me.

Gal. 2:9b

the grace
that was given unto me,

I Cor. 2:10a

But unto us God revealed them through the
Spirit:

Gal. 1:12

For neither did I receive it from man, nor
was I taught it, but it came to me through
revelation of Jesus Christ. Cf. Gal. 1:16.
Cf. Rom. 11:25; I Cor. 2:7; 4:1 of the mystery

I Cor. 5:9a

I wrote unto you in my epistle
Cf. Gal. 1:12, 16; 2:2, 7, 8

II Cor. 11:6b

yet am I not in knowledge;
nay, in every way have we
made this manifest unto you in all things.

I Cor. 2:7, 8a

but we speak God's wisdom
in a mystery,

even the wisdom that hath been hidden . . .
which none of the rulers of this world
hath known:

I Thess. 2:18; Cf. Gal. 5:2

I Paul

I Cor. 1:4b; cf. Rom. 12:6; 15:15

the grace of God
which was given
you in Christ Jesus;

Rom. 16:25b; cf. Gal. 2:2b

according to the revelation

Rom. 16:25b, 26a

of the mystery

which hath been kept in silence
through times eternal,

EPHESIANS	COLOSSIAN PARALLELS
3	
unto the sons of men,[1]	
as it hath now been revealed	but now hath it been manifested
unto his holy apostles	to his saints,
and prophets	
	1:8
	who also declared unto us your love
in the Spirit;	in the Spirit.
6 to wit, that the Gentiles are	
fellow-heirs,	
and fellow-members of the body,	
and fellow-partakers of the promise	
in Christ Jesus	
through the gospel,	

---

1. Cf. Mk. 3:28.

OTHER PAULINE PARALLELS

Cf. I Cor. 2:10 above
I Cor. 12:28b
first apostles
secondly prophets,

I Cor. 14:16a
Else if thou bless with the spirit,
Cf. I Cor. 2:10 above
Rom. 8:17b
heirs of God, and joint-heirs with Christ;
Rom. 12:5a
so we, who are many, are one
body in Christ,

Rom. 4:13, 14, 16, 17
For not through the law was the promise to
Abraham or to his seed that he should be heir of
the world, but through the righteousness
of faith. For if they that are of the law are
heirs, faith is made void, and the promise
is made of none effect: . . . For this cause
it is of faith, that it may be according to
grace; to the end that the promise may be
sure to all the seed; not to that only which
is of the law, but to that also which is of
the faith of Abraham, who is the father of
us all (as it is written, A father of many
nations have I made thee) before him whom
he believed, even God, who giveth life to the
dead, and calleth the things that are not, as
though they were.
II Thess. 2:14b
through our gospel,

but now is manifested,

Rom. 16:26b
and by the scriptures of the
prophets . . . is made known unto
all the nations

Gal. 3:26-29
For ye are all sons of God, through
faith in Christ Jesus. For as many of
you as were baptized into Christ did
put on Christ. There can be neither
Jew nor Greek, there can be neither
bond nor free, there can be no male
and female; for ye are all one man in
Christ Jesus. And if ye are Christ's,
then are ye Abraham's seed, heirs according to promise.

EPHESIANS	COLOSSIAN PARALLELS
3	**1:23b**
7 whereof I was made a minister,	whereof I Paul was made a minister.
	1:25
according to the gift of that grace of God which was given me	whereof I was made a minister, according to the dispensation of God which was given me
	1:29b
according to the working of his power.	according to his working which worketh in me mightily
8 Unto me, who am less than the least of all saints,	
was this grace given,	
	1:27
to preach unto the Gentiles	to whom God was pleased to make known
the unsearchable riches of Christ;	what is the riches of the glory of this mystery among the Gentiles . . . which is Christ in you, the hope of glory:
	1:25b, 26
9 and to make all men see	
what is the dispensation	whereof I was made a minister, according to the dispensation of God, . . . to fulfil the word of God,
of the mystery which for ages hath been hid	even the mystery which hath been hid for ages and generations:
	3:3b
	your life is hid with Christ
in God	in God.
	1:16b
who created all things;	all things have been created through him (cf. 1:27 above)
10 to the intent that now	

OTHER PAULINE PARALLELS

Rom. 5:15b

Rom. 12:3; cf. 6

the grace of God,
and the gift by the grace
of the one man, Jesus Christ,
abound unto the many.

For I say, through the grace
that was given me,

I Cor. 15:9a

For I am
the least of the apostles, that am not
meet to be called an apostle,

Gal. 2:7b

that I had been intrusted

Gal. 1:15b

and called me through his grace,
See Rom. 5:15b and 12:3 above

Gal. 1:16b

that I might preach him among the Gentiles;

with the gospel of the uncircumcision,

Rom. 11:33

O the depth of the riches both of the wisdom
and the knowledge of God! how unsearchable
are his judgments, and his ways past tracing
out!

I Cor. 2:7

but we speak God's wisdom

Rom. 16:25b, 26

according to the revelation

in a mystery, even the wisdom
that hath been hidden, which God
foreordained before the worlds unto our
glory:

of the mystery
which hath been kept in silence
through times eternal,

Rom. 11:36a

For of him, and through him, and
unto him, are all things.

but now is manifested, and

EPHESIANS	COLOSSIAN PARALLELS
3	1:16c
unto the principalities	principalities
and the powers	or powers;
	1:16b
in the heavenly <u>places</u>	in the heavens
might be made known	Cf. 1:27 above
through the church	
the manifold wisdom of God,	

11 according to the eternal purpose
which he purposed

in Christ Jesus our Lord:
12 in whom we have boldness
and access

in confidence
through our faith in him.
13 Wherefore I ask
that ye may not faint

1:24a

Now I rejoice
in my sufferings for your sake,

2:1

at my tribulations for you,

For I would have you know how greatly I
strive for you, and for them at Laodicea,
and for as many as have not seen my face
in the flesh,

which are your glory.
14 For this cause
I bow my knees unto the Father,

OTHER PAULINE PARALLELS

Cf. Rom. 8:38

by the scriptures of the prophets,
according to the commandment of the
eternal God,

is made known unto all the nations,

II Cor. 8:18b
through all the churches;

unto obedience of faith.

See Rom. 11:33 above

I Cor. 2:7
but we speak God's wisdom in
a mystery, even the wisdom that
hath been hidden,

Rom. 8:28b
even to them that are called
according to his purpose.

which God foreordained before
the worlds unto our glory:

Rom. 5:1b, 2
through our Lord Jesus Christ;
through whom also
we have had our access

II Cor. 3:12
Having therefore such a hope,
we use great boldness of speech,
II Cor. 3:4
And such confidence have we
through Christ to God-ward:

by faith into this grace wherein we stand:
II Cor. 4:1b, 16
we faint not: . . . Wherefore we faint not;

I Thess. 2:20a
For ye are our glory
Rom. 14:11b; Isa. 45:23
"to me every knee shall bow"
Cf. Phil. 2:10

EPHESIANS	COLOSSIAN PARALLELS
3	
15 from whom every² family	1:16b
in heaven and on earth	in the heavens and upon the earth,
is named,	
16 that he would grant you,	1:27b; cf. 1:11a
according to	to make known
the riches of his glory,	what is the riches of the glory
	of this mystery
that ye may be strengthened	
with power	
through his Spirit	
in the inward man;	
	1:19; cf. 2:9
17 that Christ may dwell	dwell;
in your hearts	
through faith;	
to the end that ye,	
being rooted and grounded	2:7a
	rooted and builded up in him,
	1:23a
	grounded and stedfast,
in love,	
18 may be strong to apprehend	2:2b, 3; cf. 1:26
	unto all riches of the full assurance of
	understanding,
with all the saints	

---

2. Cf. Acts 3:25.

OTHER PAULINE PARALLELS

I Cor. 8:5b
whether in heaven or on earth;
Rom. 15:20b
not where Christ was <u>already</u> named,
Rom. 9:23a
that he might make known
the riches of his glory
I Cor. 16:13b
quit you like men, be strong.
Rom. 15:13b, 19b
in the power
of the Holy Spirit.
Rom. 7:22
after the inward man:
II Cor. 4:16b
but though our outward man is decaying,
yet our inward man is renewed day by day.
Rom. 8:9b
if so be that the Spirit of
God dwelleth in you.
I Cor. 3:16b
and <u>that</u> the Spirit of God dwelleth in you?
II Cor. 1:22b; cf. 13:5
and gave <u>us</u> the earnest of the Spirit
in our hearts.

II Cor. 13:5b
that Jesus Christ is

in you?

I Cor. 9:24b
Even so run; that ye may attain.

II Cor. 1:1b
with all the saints that are in the whole
of Achaia:

EPHESIANS	COLOSSIAN PARALLELS
3	
what is the breadth and length	that they may know the mystery of God, <u>even</u> Christ,
and height and depth,	
19 and to know	in whom are all the treasures of wisdom and knowledge hidden.
the love of Christ	
which passeth knowledge,	
	1:9b
that ye may be filled	that ye may be filled
	2:9, 10a
unto all the fulness of God.	for in him dwelleth all the fulness of the Godhead bodily, and in him ye are made full,
20 Now unto him that is able	
to do exceeding abundantly above all that we ask or think,	
	1:29b
according to the power that worketh in us,	according to his working, which worketh in me mightily.
21 unto him <u>be</u> the glory	
in the church	
and in Christ Jesus	
	1:26b
unto all generations for ever and ever. Amen.	for ages and generations:

OTHER PAULINE PARALLELS

Rom. 8:39a
nor height, nor depth,
II Cor. 9:14
by reason of the exceeding grace of God in
you.
I Cor. 8:1
Knowledge puffeth up, but love edifieth.
I Cor. 13:2, 8
And if I have the gift of prophecy, and know
all mysteries and all knowledge: and if I have
all faith, so as to remove mountains, but
have not love, I am nothing. . . . Love never
faileth: . . . whether there be knowledge, it
shall be done away.

Rom. 8:35a
Who shall separate us

from the love of Christ?

Rom. 16:25a
Now to him that is able to establish you
I Thess. 3:10b
praying exceedingly

Gal. 3:5b; cf. Phil. 3:21
and worketh miracles among you,
Rom. 11:36b; cf. 16:27
To him be the glory
I Cor. 6:4b
in the church
Rom. 3:24b
in Christ Jesus:

Gal. 1:5a
to whom be the glory
I Cor. 7:17b
in all the churches.

Rom. 11:36c; cf. 16:27c
for ever. Amen.

Gal. 1:5b; Phil. 4:20
for ever and ever. Amen.

EPHESIANS	COLOSSIAN PARALLELS

4

1 I therefore,

the prisoner in the Lord,

beseech you

	1:10a
to walk worthily	to walk worthily
of the calling wherewith ye	of the Lord
were called,	

	3:12, 13a
2 with all lowliness	Put on therefore . . . lowliness,
and meekness,	meekness,
with longsuffering,	longsuffering;
forbearing one another	forbearing one another,
	3:14, 15
	and above all these things
in love;	put on love, which is
3 giving diligence to keep	
the unity of the Spirit	
in the bond	the bond of perfectness.
of peace.	And let the peace of Christ
	rule in your hearts, to the which
4 There is one body,	also ye were called in one body;

and one Spirit,

even as also ye were called
in one hope of your calling;

(See below)

5 one Lord, one faith,
one baptism,

6 one God and Father of all,

who is over all, and through all,

OTHER PAULINE PARALLELS

Rom. 12:1a
I beseech you therefore,
Philem. 1, cf. 9
a prisoner of Christ Jesus,

(See above)
I Thess. 2:12b
that ye should walk worthily
of God, who calleth you

Phil. 2:3b
but in lowliness of mind

each counting other better than himself;
Phil. 2:2b
that ye be of the same mind,
having the same love,

being of one accord, of one mind:

I Cor. 10:17b
we who are many, are
one bread, one body:
I Cor. 12:13
For in one Spirit were we all
baptized into one body . . . and were
all made to drink of one Spirit.
I Cor. 7:20
Let each man abide in that calling
wherein he was called.
I Cor. 8:6a
yet to us there is one God, the Father, of
whom are all things, and we unto him;
and one Lord, Jesus Christ,
See I Cor. 12:13 above; cf. 1:13
Rom. 3:30a
if so be that God is one,
Rom. 11:36a
For of him, and through him,

II Cor. 10:1a
Now I Paul myself
Phil. 1:13b
my bonds in Christ
II Cor. 10:1a
entreat you
II Thess. 1:11b
that our God may count you worthy
of your calling,

I Thess. 4:9b
to love one another:

Rom. 12:4a, 5a
For even as we have many
members in one body, . . . who are
many, are one in Christ,
Cf. I Cor. 12:4

Cf. I Cor. 12:6

Rom. 9:5b
who is over all, God

EPHESIANS	COLOSSIAN PARALLELS
4	

and in all.

7 But unto each one of us
was the grace given
according to the measure

of the gift of Christ.

8 Wherefore he saith,   Cf. 2:15
When he ascended on high, he led captivity
captive, and gave gifts unto men.[1]
9 (Now this, He ascended, what is
it but that he also descended
into the lower parts of the earth?
10 He that descended is the same
also that ascended far above all the
heavens,   1:19, 20
that he **might** fill all things.)   that in him should all the fulness dwell;
                                              and through him to reconcile all things
                                              unto himself,

11 And he gave

some to be apostles;
and some, prophets;
and some, evangelists;[2]

and some, pastors and teachers;[3]

12 for the perfecting of the saints,
unto the work of ministering,

unto the building up

------

1. Ps. 68:18: Thou hast ascended on
high, thou has led away captives; Thou
has received gifts among men.

2. Acts 21:8b: Philip the evangelist.

3. Acts 20:28: to feed the church of
the Lord.

OTHER PAULINE PARALLELS

and unto him, are all things.
     Rom. 12:6a
And having gifts differing
according to the grace that
was given to us,
     Rom. 5:15b
the gift by the grace of
the one man, Jesus Christ,

                                  Cf. I Cor. 12:7-11
                                  Cf. Rom. 12:3

     Rom. 10:6b, 7
Who shall ascend into heaven?
(that is, to bring Christ down:)

or, Who shall descend into the abyss? (that
is, to bring Christ up from the dead.)
     II Cor. 12:2b
such a one caught up even to the third heaven.

     I Cor. 12:28a
And God hath set some in the church,
     (Cf. I Cor. 12:5)
first apostles,
secondly prophets,

thirdly teachers,
     II Cor. 13:9b
this we also pray for, even your perfecting.

     II Cor. 12:19c
But all things, beloved, <u>are</u> for
your edifying.

     Rom. 12:6-8b
And having gifts differing according
to the grace that was given to us,

whether prophecy, <u>let us prophesy</u>
according to the proportion of our faith;
or ministry, <u>let us give ourselves</u> to
our ministry;
or he that teacheth, to his teaching;
or he that exhorteth, to his exhorting:

     See Rom. 12:7 above
     I Cor. 14:26b
Let all things be done
unto edifying.

EPHESIANS	COLOSSIAN PARALLELS
4	

of the body of Christ;

13 till we all attain

unto the unity of the faith,

and of the knowledge
of the Son of God,

	1:28b
	that we may present
unto a fullgrown man,	every man perfect in Christ:
	2:9, 10a
unto the measure of the stature	for in him dwelleth
of the fulness of Christ:	all the fulness of the Godhead . . .
	and in him ye are made full,
	2:8
14 that we may be no longer children,	Take heed lest there shall
	be any one
tossed to and fro	that maketh spoil of you
and carried about	
with every wind of doctrine,	through his philosophy and vain deceit,
by the sleight of men,	after the tradition of men,
in craftiness,	
after the wiles of error;	after the rudiments of the world,
	and not after Christ:
15 but speaking truth in love,	
	1:10b
may grow up in all things into him,	bearing fruit in every good work, and increasing in the knowledge of God:
	1:18a
who is the head,	And he is the head of the body,
	the church:
	2:19a
even Christ;	and not holding fast the Head,
16 from whom all the body	from whom all the body,
fitly framed	being supplied

OTHER PAULINE PARALLELS

I Cor. 12:27a

Now ye are the body of Christ,

Phil. 3:11

if by any means I may attain
unto the resurrection from the dead.

Philem. 6

that the fellowship of thy faith
may become effectual,
in the knowledge of every good thing
which is in you, unto Christ.

Gal. 2:20b

the Son of God

I Cor. 2:6a

We speak wisdom, however,
among them that are fullgrown:

(See below)

I Cor. 3:1b

as unto babes in Christ.

I Cor. 14:20

Brethren, be not children in
mind: yet in malice be ye
babes, but in mind be men.

Gal. 4:16

So then am I become your enemy,
by telling you the truth?

I Cor. 11:3b

the head of every man

is Christ:

EPHESIANS	COLOSSIAN PARALLELS
4	
and knit together	and knit together
through that which every joint supplieth,	through the joints and bands,
	1:29b
according to the working	striving according to his working,
in due measure	
of each several part,	
	2:19b
maketh the increase of the body	increaseth with the increase of God.
unto the building up of itself in love.	
	2:4a; cf. 2:6 below
17 This I say therefore,	This I say,
and testify in the Lord,	
	3:7
that ye no longer walk	wherein ye also once walked,
as the Gentiles also walk,	when ye lived in these things;
in the vanity of their mind,	
	1:21a
18 being darkened in their understanding,	And you, being in time past alienated
alienated from the life of God,	
because of the ignorance that is in them,	
because of the hardening	
of their heart;	
19 who being past feeling	
gave themselves up to	
lasciviousness,	**3:5b**
to work all uncleanness	uncleanness . . .
with greediness.	and covetousness . . .
	2:6, 7
20 But ye did not so learn	As therefore ye received
Christ;	Christ Jesus the Lord,
21 if so be that ye heard him,	
and were taught in him,	so walk in him, . . .
	even as ye were taught,
even as truth is in Jesus:	

OTHER PAULINE PARALLELS

Phil. 3:21
according to the working

II Thess. 2:9b
according to the working
of Satan

I Cor. 14:12b
unto the edifying of the church

I Cor. 10:8b; 13:10b
for building up

Cf. Rom. 1:18-32
Gal. 5:3a
Yea, I testify again

Rom. 8:20a
For, the creation was subjected to vanity,
Rom. 1:21b
but became vain in their reasonings,
and their senseless heart was darkened.
Rom. 10:3a
For being ignorant of God's righteousness,
Rom. 11:25b
a hardening in part
hath befallen Israel.
Rom. 1:24a
Wherefore God gave them up in the
lusts of their hearts
unto uncleanness,

(See below)
II Cor. 12:21b
of the uncleanness and fornication
and lasciviousness which they had
committed.

II Cor. 11:10a
As the truth of Christ is in me,

Rom. 9:1a
I say the truth in Christ,

EPHESIANS	COLOSSIAN PARALLELS
4	3:8a, 9b
22 that ye put away,	but now do ye also put them all away: . . .
(See 24 below) as concerning your former manner of life,	
	seeing that ye have put off
the old man,	the old man
that waxeth corrupt	
after the lusts of deceit;	with his doings,
23 and that ye be renewed	(See below) 2:18b
in the spirit of your mind,	by his fleshly mind,
	3:10
24 and put on the new man,	and have put on the new man that is being renewed unto knowledge
that after God hath been created	after the image of him that
in righteousness and holiness of	created him:
truth.[4]	3:8a
25 Wherefore, putting away	but now do ye also put them all away:
	3:9a
falsehood,	lie not one to another:
speak ye truth	
each one with his neighbor:[5]	
for we are members one of another.	
	3:8b
26 Be ye angry, and sin not:[6]	anger, wrath,
let not the sun go down upon your wrath:	

---

4. Lk. 1:75a: in holiness and right-eousness.

5. Zech. 8:16b: Speak ye every man the truth with his neighbor;

6. Ps. 4:4a: Sept., Be ye angry, and sin not:

OTHER PAULINE PARALLELS

Cf. Rom. 8:13; Gal. 6:8

Rom. 13:12b
Let us therefore cast off the
works of darkness,
and let us put on the armor of light.

Gal. 1:13a
my manner of life in time past

Rom. 6:6
our old man
Rom. 6:12b
that ye should obey the lusts thereof:
Rom. 12:2b
be ye transformed by the renewing

of your mind,
Gal. 3:27b
did put on Christ.

II Cor. 11:3a
But I fear, lest by any means,
as the serpent beguiled Eve . . .
your minds should be corrupted

Rom. 13:14a; cf. 12b
But put ye on the Lord Jesus Christ,
Rom. 6:4b
so we also might walk in newness of
life.
Rom. 13:12b
let us therefore cast off
the works of darkness,

Rom. 12:5
So we, . . . are one body in Christ, and
severally members one of another.
I Cor. 15:34a
Awake to soberness righteously
and sin not;
(See below)
Rom. 12:19b
But give place unto the wrath of God:

EPHESIANS	COLOSSIAN PARALLELS

4

27 neither give place

to the devil.[7]

28 Let him that stole steal no more:

but rather let him labor,

working
with his hands

the thing that is good,

that he may have whereof to give

to him that hath need.

	3:8
	but now do ye also put them all away . . .
29 Let no corrupt speech	railing, shameful speaking
proceed out of your mouth,	out of your mouth: (cf. 4:6 below)
but such as is good	

for edifying as the need may be,
that it may give grace to them that hear.
30 And grieve not

the Holy Spirit of God,[8]

in whom ye were sealed

---

7. Acts 13:10b: thou son of the devil,
8. Isa. 63:10: his holy Spirit.

OTHER PAULINE PARALLELS

II Cor. 2:11
that no advantage may be gained over us
by Satan: for we are not ignorant of his
devices.

Rom. 2:21b
thou that preachest a man should not steal,
dost thou steal?

I Cor. 4:12a
and we toil,

Rom. 2:10b
to every man that
worketh

Gal. 7:10b
let us
work

I Thess. 4:11b, 12b
working
with our own
hands:

to work
with your hands,

Gal. 6:10b
that which is good
toward all men,

good,

Rom. 12:13a
communicating to
the
necessities of the
saints;

. . . that ye . . .

may have need of
nothing.

II Thess. 2:17b
in every good work and word.

I Cor. 14:26b
Let all things be done unto edifying.

I Thess. 5:19
Quench not the spirit:

I Thess. 4:8b
God, who giveth his Holy Spirit
unto you.

Rom. 8:23b, d
who have the first fruits
of the Spirit, . . .

II Cor. 1:22
who also sealed us, and gave us
the earnest of the Spirit in our hearts.

waiting for our adoption,

EPHESIANS	COLOSSIAN PARALLELS
4	
unto the day of redemption.[9]	3:8
	but now do ye also put
	them all away:
31 Let all bitterness,	anger, wrath, malice,
and wrath, and anger,	railing, shameful speaking
and clamor, and railing.	out of your mouth:
be put away from you,	(See above)
with all malice:	3:12, 13
	Put on therefore, . . .
32 and be ye kind one to another,	a heart of compassion, kindness, . . .
tenderhearted,	. . . and forgiving each other, . . .
forgiving each other,	even as the Lord
even as God also	forgave you, so also do ye:
in Christ forgave you.	

9. Isa. 49:8b: a day of salvation.

OTHER PAULINE PARALLELS

II Cor. 6:2b

"in a day of salvation."

<u>to wit</u>, the redemption of our body.

I Cor. 5:2b

might be taken away from among you.

EPHESIANS	COLOSSIAN PARALLELS
5	3:12a
1 Be ye therefore imitators of God,	Put on therefore as God's elect,
as beloved children;	holy and beloved,
2 and walk in love,	
even as Christ also loved you, and gave himself up for us,	
an offering and a sacrifice to God[1]	
for an odor of a sweet smell.[2]	3:5a Put to death therefore your members which are upon the earth: fornication, uncleanness, passion, evil desire and covetousness,
3 But fornication, and all uncleanness,	
or covetousness, let it not even be named among you,	
as becometh saints;	3:8 but now do ye also put them all away: . . . shameful speaking out of your mouth:
4 nor filthiness, nor foolish talking, or jesting,	
which are not befitting:	3:18b as is fitting in the Lord.
but rather giving of thanks.	2:7b abounding in thanksgiving. 3:15b and be ye thankful. 3:17b giving thanks to God the Father through him.
5 For this ye know of a surety,	

---

1. Ps. 40:6a: sacrifice and offering.
2. Ezek. 20:41a: as a sweet savor.

OTHER PAULINE PARALLELS

I Cor. 4:16b
be ye imitators of me.

I Cor. 11:1
Be ye imitators of me,
even as I also am of Christ.

I Cor. 4:14b
to admonish you
as my beloved children.

Rom. 14:15b
thou walkest no longer in love.

Gal. 2:20b
the Son of God, who loved me,
and gave himself up for me.

Phil. 4:18b
an odor of a sweet smell,
a sacrifice acceptable,
well-pleasing to God.

(See above)

II Cor. 12:21b; cf. Rom. 1:24-32
of the uncleanness and fornication
and lasciviousness

I Cor. 5:11b
if any man that is named a brother
be a fornicator, or covetous, or an idolater,

Rom. 1:28b
to do those things
which are not fitting;

I Thess. 5:18a
in everything give thanks:

I Cor. 6:9a
Or know ye not

I Cor. 6:9b, 10b
Be not deceived:

EPHESIANS	COLOSSIAN PARALLELS
5	3:5b
that no fornicator, nor unclean person,	fornication, uncleanness, . . .
nor covetous man,	and covetousness,
who is an idolater,	which is idolatry;
hath any inheritance	
in the kingdom	
of Christ and God.	2:4b
6 Let no man deceive you	that no one may delude you
with empty words:	with persuasiveness of speech.
	2:8a
	Take heed lest there shall be anyone
	that maketh spoil of you through his
	philosophy and vain deceit,
	3:6
for because of these things	for which things' sake
cometh the wrath of God	cometh the wrath of God
upon the sons of disobedience.	upon the sons of disobedience:
7 Be not ye therefore partakers with them;	
8 for ye were once darkness,	
but are now light in the Lord:	
walk as children of light	Cf. 1:12
9 (for the fruit of the light	
is in all goodness	
and righteousness and truth),	

OTHER PAULINE PARALLELS

		Gal. 5:19b-21
that the unrighteous	neither fornicators	fornication, un-cleanness, las-civiousness,
	nor idolaters,	idolatry, . . .
	nor adulterers, . . .	
	nor covetous . . .	they who practise such things
shall not inherit the kingdom of God?	shall inherit the kingdom of God.	shall not inherit the kingdom of God.

Rom. 1:18a
For the wrath of God
is revealed from heaven
against all ungodliness and unrighteous-
ness of men,

II Cor. 6:14
Be not unequally yoked with unbelievers:
for what fellowship have righteousness
and iniquity? or what communion
hath light with darkness?

Rom. 2:19b; cf. II Cor. 6:14
a light of them that are in darkness,

I Thess. 5:5; cf. Rom. 13:12
for ye are all sons of light,
and sons of the day:

Gal. 5:22, 23a
But the fruit of the spirit
is love, joy, peace,
longsuffering, kindness, goodness,
faithfulness, meakness, self-control;

Rom. 13:12b, 13a
let us therefore cast off
the works of darkness,
and let us put on the armor of light.

Let us walk becomingly,
as in the day;

EPHESIANS	COLOSSIAN PARALLELS
5	
10 proving	3:20b
what is well-pleasing unto the Lord;	for this is well-pleasing in the Lord.
11 and have no fellowship	
with the unfruitful works of darkness,	
but rather even reprove them;	
12 for the things which are done by them	3:8a
in secret	but now do ye also put them all away
it is a shame even to speak of.	. . . shameful speaking out of your mouth:
13 But all things when they are reproved	
are made manifest by the light:[3]	
for everything that is made manifest	
is light.	
14 Wherefore <u>he</u> saith,	
Awake, thou that sleepest,	
and rise from the dead,	
and Christ shall shine upon thee.	
15 Look therefore carefully how	
	4:5
ye walk,	Walk
not as unwise,	
but as wise;	in wisdom toward them
	that are without,
16 redeeming the time,	redeeming the time.
because the days are evil.	
17 Wherefore	Cf. 1:9

---

3. Cf. Lk. 11:34-36.

OTHER PAULINE PARALLELS

Rom. 12:2b

that ye may prove
what is the good and acceptable and perfect
will of God.

Phil. 4:18b

well-pleasing to God

II Cor. 6:14b

or what communion hath light
with darkness?

Rom. 13:12b

let us therefore cast off the
works of darkness,

Cf. Rom. 1:24, 26, 27

Cf. I Cor. 11:6; 14:35
I Cor. 14:24b, 25a

he is reproved by all, he is judged by all,

the secrets of his heart are made manifest;

I Cor. 4:5b

who will both bring to light the hidden
things of darkness,
and will make manifest the counsels
of the hearts;

I Cor. 3:10b

But let each man take heed how he
buildeth thereon.

Rom. 13:13a

Let us walk becomingly,
as in the day;

Rom. 16:19b

but I would have you wise
unto that which is good,

Gal. 1:4b

that he might deliver us out
of this present evil world,

Cf. Rom. 1:26; I Cor. 4:17, etc.

Look [this Greek word and form is
found ten times in the Letters of Paul]

EPHESIANS	COLOSSIAN PARALLELS
5	
be ye not foolish,	
	4:12b
but understand	and fully assured
what the will of the Lord is.	in all the will of God.
18 And be not drunken with wine,[4]	
wherein is riot,[5]	
but be filled with the Spirit;[6]	3:16b, 17
19 speaking one to another	teaching and admonishing one another
in psalms and hymns	with psalms and hymns
and spiritual songs,	and spiritual songs,
singing and making melody	singing
with your heart	with grace in your hearts
to the Lord;	unto God.
20 giving thanks	(See below)
always for all things	and whatsoever ye do,
	in word or in deed, do all
in the name of our Lord Jesus Christ	in the name of the Lord Jesus,
to God, even the Father;	giving thanks to God the Father through him.
21 subjecting yourselves	
one to another	
in the fear of Christ.	3:18
22 Wives, be in subjection	Wives, be in subjection
unto your own husbands,	to your husbands,
as unto the Lord.	as is fitting in the Lord.
23 For the husband is the head	
of the wife,	

---

4. Prov. 23:31a: Sept. Be not drunken with wines.

5. Lk. 15:13: with riotous living.

6. Lk. 4:1; Acts 7:55; etc.: full of the Holy Spirit.

OTHER PAULINE PARALLELS

Cf. II Cor. 12:11a

I am become foolish:

Gal. 3:3a

Are ye so foolish?

Rom. 2:17b, 18a

and gloriest in God, and knowest
his will,

Rom. 12:2b

that ye may prove
what is the good and perfect and acceptable will of God.

I Thess. 5:7b

and they that are drunken are drunken
in the night.

Cf. Rom. 13:13b

not in revelling and drunkenness,

I Cor. 14:15b

I will sing with the spirit,
and I will sing with the understanding also.

I Thess. 5:18a

in everything give thanks:

Phil. 1:3, 4

I thank my God . . .
always . . . on behalf of you all

Gal. 5:13b

but through love be servants
one to another

Phil. 2:3b

each counting other better
than himself; [7]

I Cor. 11:3b; cf. 14:34

the head of every man is Christ;
and the head of the woman is
the man;

---

7. Cf. Rom. 12:10b.

EPHESIANS	COLOSSIAN PARALLELS
5	1:18
as Christ also is the head	And he is the head of the body,
of the church,	the church:
being himself the saviour of the body.	
24 But as the church is subject to Christ,	
so let the wives also be	Cf. 3:18 above
to their husbands in everything.	3:19
25 Husbands love your wives,	Husbands, love your wives,
	and be not bitter against them.
even as Christ also loved the church,	
and gave himself up for it;	
26 that he might sanctify it,	
having cleansed it	
by the washing of water	
with the word,	
	1:22b
27 that he might present the church	to present you
to himself a glorious church,	
not having spot or wrinkle	
or any such thing;	
but that it should be	
holy and without blemish.	holy and without blemish
	and unreprovable before him:
	3:19a
28 Even so ought husbands also	Husbands,
to love their own wives	love your wives,
as their own bodies.	
He that loveth his own wife	
loveth himself:	
29 for no man ever hated his own flesh;	

OTHER PAULINE PARALLELS

I Cor. 12:27a

Now ye are the body of Christ,

(See above)

Phil. 3:20b

whence also we wait for a Saviour,
the Lord Jesus Christ:

Gal. 2:20b

the Son of God, who loved me,
and gave himself up for me.

See below. Cf. II Cor. 7:1b

I Cor. 6:11b

but ye were washed, but ye were sanctified,

Rom. 10:9a

because if thou shalt confess with thy
mouth Jesus as Lord,

II Cor. 11:2b

for I espoused you to one husband,
that I might present you
as a pure virgin to Christ.

I Cor. 7:3, 4

Let the husband render unto the wife her
due: and likewise also the wife unto the
husband.
The wife hath not power
over her own body, but the husband: and
likewise also the husband hath not power
over
his own body, but the wife.

Cf. I Cor. 6:16 below

EPHESIANS	COLOSSIAN PARALLELS

5

but nourisheth and cherisheth it,

even as Christ also the church;

30 because we are members of his body.

31 For this cause shall a man leave
his father and mother,
and shall cleave to his wife;
and the two shall become one flesh.[8]

32 This mystery is great:

but I speak in regard of Christ
and of the church.
33 Nevertheless do ye also severally

love each one his own wife

even as himself;

	3:18a, 20, 21
and let the wife see that she fear her husband.	Wives, be in subjection to your husbands,

---

8. Gen. 2:24.

OTHER PAULINE PARALLELS

I Thess. 2:7b

as when a nurse cherisheth her
own children:

I Cor. 6:15a

Know ye not that your bodies are
members of Christ?

I Cor. 12:27

Now ye are the body of Christ,
and severally members thereof.

Rom. 12:5

so we, who are many, are one body in
Christ, and severally members one
of another.

I Cor. 6:16b

For, The twain, saith he, shall become one
flesh.

Rom. 11:25a

For I would not . . . have you
ignorant of this mystery,

I Cor. 15:51a

Behold, I tell you a mystery:

I Cor. 11:11a

Nevertheless, neither is the woman
without the man,

Rom. 12:5b

severally

I Cor. 7:2b

let each man have his own wife,

Rom. 13:9b; Gal. 5:14b

Thou shalt love thy neighbor
as thyself.

Cf. I Cor. 11:3b

and the head of the woman is the man.

EPHESIANS	COLOSSIAN PARALLELS
6	3:20

1 Children,	Children,
obey your parents	obey your parents in all things
in the Lord:	(See below)
for this is right.	for this is well-pleasing
	in the Lord.
2 Honor thy father and mother	
(which is the first commandment	
with promise),	
3 that it may be well with thee,	3:21
and thou mayest live long on the earth.[1]	
4 And, ye fathers,	Fathers,
provoke not your children to wrath:	provoke not your children,
but nurture them	that they be not discouraged.
in the chastening	Cf. 3:16c
and admonition of the Lord.[2]	3:22a
5 Servants,	Servants,
be obedient unto them	obey in all things them
that according to the flesh	that are your masters
are your masters,	according to the flesh: . . .
with fear and trembling,	fearing the Lord:
in singleness of your heart,	(See below)
	3:23b
as unto Christ;	as unto the Lord,
	3:22b
6 not in the way of eyeservice,	not with eye-service,
as men-pleasers;	as men-pleasers,
but	but in singleness of heart,
	3:24b
as servants of Christ,	ye serve the Lord Christ.

---

1. Deut. 5:16: Honor thy father and thy mother, . . . that thy days may be long, and that it may go well with thee, in the land. . . . Cf. Exod. 20:12a

2. Prov. 3:11: the chastening of Jehovah, . . . his reproof.

OTHER PAULINE PARALLELS

I Cor. 4:14b
to admonish you
as my beloved children.

Phil. 2:12b, c
even as ye have always obeyed, . . .

Rom. 6:16b
his servants ye are
whom ye obey;

II Cor. 7:15b; cf. I Cor. 2:3
with fear and trembling:
with fear and trembling

Gal. 1:10b
or am I striving to please men?
if I were still pleasing men,

I should not be a servant of Christ.

EPHESIANS 6	COLOSSIAN PARALLELS
	3:22c-25a
doing the will of God	fearing the Lord:
from the heart;	whatsoever ye do, work heartily,
7 with good will doing service,	
as unto the Lord,	as unto the Lord,
and not unto men:	and not unto men:
8 knowing that whatsoever	knowing that
good thing	
each one doeth,	
the same shall he receive again	from the Lord
from the Lord,	ye shall receive
	the recompence of the inheritance: . . .
	For he that doeth wrong shall
	receive again for the wrong
	that he hath done:
whether he be bond or free.	
	4:1
9 And, ye masters,	Masters,
do the same things unto them,	render unto your servants
	that which is just and equal:
and forbear threatening:	
knowing that	
he who is both their Master and yours	
is in heaven,	
and there is no respect of persons	
with him.	
10 Finally,	
	1:11a
be strong in the Lord,	strengthened with all power,
and in the strength of his might.	according to the might
	of his glory,

OTHER PAULINE PARALLELS

Cf. I Cor. 7:22b

he that was called being free, is
Christ's bondservant.

Rom. 12:2b

the . . . will of God.

Gal. 2:10b

let us work that which is good
toward all men,

(See below)

II Cor. 5:10b

that each one may receive the
things <u>done</u> in the body,

according to what he hath done,

Gal. 3:28b

there can be neither bond nor free,

Cf. I Cor. 12:13b

whether bond or free;

whether <u>it be</u> good or bad.

Rom. 2:11

for there is no respect of persons
with God.

Gal. 6:17a

Henceforth

Phil. 3:1a

Finally,

Rom. 4:20b

(Cf. I Cor. 16:13)

Phil. 4:13

I can do all things in him that strength-
eneth me.

II Thess. 1:9b

and from the glory of his might,

but waxed strong through faith,

EPHESIANS	COLOSSIAN PARALLELS

EPHESIANS
6

11 Put on the whole armor of God,[3]

that ye may be able to stand

against the wiles of the devil.

12 For our wrestling is not

                                          1:16b

against flesh and blood,   things visible and things invisible,
                                          whether thrones or dominions

but against the principalities,   or principalities

against the powers,[4]   or powers: (cf. 2:15)

against the world-rulers

of this darkness,

against the spiritual <u>hosts</u> of wicked-
ness[5]
in the heavenly <u>places</u>.   3:12a
13 Wherefore take up   Put on therefore,
the whole armor of God,
                                          4:12b
that ye may be able to withstand[6]   that ye may stand perfect
in the evil day,
and, having done all, to stand.[7]   and fully assured in all the will of God.

---

3. Lk. 11:22b: whole armor;
cf. Wisdom 5:17a.

4. Principalities . . . powers: the
same Greek words appear in Lk. 12:11
("rulers . . . authorities," ASV).

5. Lk. 8:2: and often: evil spirits.

6. See on vs. 11 above.

7. Lk. 21:15b: able to withstand.

OTHER PAULINE PARALLELS

Rom. 13:12b; cf. 14
and let us put on the armor of light.

I Cor. 16:13
Watch ye, stand fast in the faith,
quit you like men, be strong.

II Cor. 2:11
that no advantage may be gained over us
by Satan: for we are not ignorant of his
devices.

I Cor. 15:50b, cf. Gal. 1:16
flesh and blood

Rom. 8:38b
nor angels, nor principalities, . . .

nor powers,

I Thess. 5:5b
we are not of the night,
nor of darkness;

I Cor. 14:1b
yet desire earnestly spiritual gifts,

Cf. I Cor. 15:40; Phil. 2:10
Rom. 13:12b
and let us put on the armor of light.

II Cor. 10:3, 4
For though we walk in the flesh,
we do not war according to the flesh
(for the weapons of our warfare
are not of the flesh,

but mighty before God to the casting
down of strongholds);
Cf. I Cor. 2:6, 8; II Thess. 2:3-7;
I Cor. 15:24

EPHESIANS	COLOSSIAN PARALLELS
6	

14 Stand therefore,
having girded your loins
with truth,[8]
and having put on
the breastplate of righteousness,[9]

See 4:12b above

15 and having shod your feet
with the preparation
of the gospel of peace;[10]

16 withal taking up
the shield of faith,[11]
wherewith ye shall be able to quench
all the fiery darts of the evil one.

3:12a, 14a

Put on therefore, . . . and above
all these things put on love,

17 And take the helmet
of salvation,[12]
and the sword of the Spirit,[13]
which is the word of God:

18 with all prayer
and supplication

4:2a

Continue stedfastly in prayer,

praying at all seasons[14]

(Cf. vs. 3 below)

---

8. Isa. 11:5: And righteousness shall be the girdle of his waist, and faithfulness the girdle of his loins.

9. Isa. 59:17a: And he put on righteousness as a breastplate.

10. Isa. 52:7b: the feet of him that bringeth good tidings, that publisheth peace.

11. Wisdom 5:19: he will take holiness for an invincible shield.

12. Isa. 59:17b: a helmet of salvation upon his head.

13. Isa. 49:2a: and he hath made my mouth like a sharp sword.

14. Lk. 18:1: they ought always to pray; 21:36: at every season, making supplication,

OTHER PAULINE PARALLELS

I Thess. 5:8b
putting on
the breastplate of faith and love;

II Thess. 3:3b
and guard you from the evil <u>one</u>.
I Thess. 5:8c
and for a helmet,
the hope of salvation.

Phil. 4:6b
in everything by prayer
by prayer and supplication
I Cor. 14:15b
I will pray

I Thess. 5:17, 18a
pray without ceasing;

in everything give thanks:

EPHESIANS	COLOSSIAN PARALLELS
6	1:8b
in the Spirit,	in the Spirit.
	4:2b-3a
and watching thereunto	watching therein
in all perseverance	with thanksgiving;
and supplication	withal praying for us also,
	1:4b
for all the saints,	toward all the saints,
	4:3b, 4
19 and on my behalf,	For us also,
that utterance may be given unto me	that God may open unto us
	a door for the word,
in opening my mouth,	(See above)
	2:15b
to make known with boldness	to speak openly
	2:2b
the mystery	the mystery the mystery
of the gospel,[15]	of Christ, of God, even Christ.
20 for which I am an ambassador	for which I am also
in chains;[16]	in bonds;
that in it I may speak boldly,	that I may make it manifest,
as I ought to speak.	as I ought to speak.
	2:1a
21 But that ye also may know	For I would have you know
	(See vs. 8 below)
	4:7, 8
my affairs, how I do,	All my affairs
Tychicus, the beloved brother	shall Tychicus
and faithful minister	(See below)
in the Lord,	

---

15. Lk. 8:10: the mysteries of the kingdom of God.

16. Acts 28:20b: I am bound with this chain.

OTHER PAULINE PARALLELS

with the spirit,	Rom. 2:29b; 8:9b; cf. II Cor. 3:6 in the spirit

       Phil. 4:22a
All the saints salute you,
      II Cor. 13:13b
All the saints salute you.
     Rom. 15:30b, 31a
for me,
that I may be delivered
      II Cor. 6:11a
Our mouth is open unto you,
      I Cor. 2:1b
proclaiming to you

the testimony [Gr. "mystery"]
of God.

     Phil. 1:20b   II Thess. 2:2b
with all boldness we waxed bold in our
                God to speak

             unto you the gospel
             of God in much conflict.

      II Cor. 5:20a
We are ambassadors therefore on behalf
of Christ,

       Philem. 9b
being such a one as Paul the aged,
and now a prisoner also of Christ
Jesus:

     I Cor. 2:12b
that we might know

     I Cor. 9:17a
for if I do this of mine own will,

EPHESIANS 6	COLOSSIAN PARALLELS
shall make known to you all things:	make known unto you, the beloved brother and faithful minister and fellow-servant in the Lord:
22 whom I have sent unto you for this very purpose, that ye may know our state, and that he may comfort your hearts.	whom I have sent unto you for this very purpose, that ye may know our state, and that he may comfort your hearts:
23 Peace be to the brethren, and love with faith, from God the Father and the Lord Jesus Christ.	
	4:18b
24 Grace be with all them that love our Lord Jesus Christ with a love incorruptible.	Grace be with you.

OTHER PAULINE PARALLELS

Philem. 12a
whom I have sent back to thee
in his own person,

Gal. 6:16
And as many as shall walk by this rule,
peace be upon them, and mercy,
and upon the Israel of God.
    (See I Cor. 16:24 below)
        II Thess. 1:2
Grace to you and peace
from God the Father
and the Lord Jesus Christ.
Cf. Rom. 1:7; I Cor. 1:3; II Cor. 1:2;
Gal. 1:3
        I Cor. 16:22-24
If any man loveth not the Lord,
let him be anathema. . . .
The grace of the Lord Jesus Christ
be with you.
My love be with you all in Christ Jesus.
        I Cor. 15:42b
it is raised in incorruption;